COUNTIN' MY BLESSINGS

COUNTIN' MY BLESSINGS

Maxine Dykes Quinton

authorHOUSE®

AuthorHouse™
1663 Liberty Drive
Bloomington, IN 47403
www.authorhouse.com
Phone: 1-800-839-8640

Published by AuthorHouse   11/26/2012

ISBN: 978-1-4772-9279-2 (sc)

CONTENTS

DEDICATION

First and foremost, I dedicate this book to my God for all the blessings He has bestowed upon me. I thank Him for talents He has given to me. May I use them to bring honor and glory to His name.

I'm thankful for my family. I have a daughter and three sons. My second son, Steve, passed away in 2009 at the age of forty-eight. I have eight grandchildren and one great grandchild as of March, 2011. I dedicate this book also to my family:

Mike and family
Leasa and family
Mark and family
And also to Steve's memory

I THANK GOD

I thank God for the ability to write,
But I don't want fortune or fame.
I just want to pen words of praise
That will glorify His name.

Just words of encouragement to the Christian
To keep on keeping on,
And to the sinner words of comfort
To know they're not alone.

And challenging words to someone
Who has fallen along the way,
If they come back to Him,
He will forgive His Word does say.

So whatever category you fall into,
Just remember God loves you,
And whatever His Word says,
That's just what He will do.

No matter what, save one,
He'll forgive if you but ask,
Just have a humble heart bowed before Him,
In His love you can bask.

As I said, I don't want fortune or fame
To call my own,
Just words to lift His name higher
And to gain Heaven's Home!!

FRONT PORCH MEDITATION

Come sit on my porch with me,
Then you'll see what all I see.

The beauty of the morning is so serene,
Each morning is different than any you've seen.

The birds say "good morning" in their own special way,
Sometimes a squirrel has something to say.

Truly one morning I disturbed a squirrel's meal,
He hung upside-down on the tree fussing, how unreal.

I only have one chair, but I can get two,
Then we can enjoy the morning together, me and you.

Perhaps you can't come sit on my porch with me,
So, why not sit on yours and very quiet be.

We both can talk to our Heavenly Father above,
Thanking Him for His Grace, Mercy and Heavenly Love!!

IT'S JUST THE RIGHT THING TO DO

If you are my sister
      or you are my brother,
Then listen;
      let's get right with one another,
For if we say we are right
      with God above,
Then our true feelings for each other
      must be Christian love,
Christian love will not allow
      envy and strife to be,
Yes, as Christians, I must love you
      and you must love me,
All little petty disagreements
      must be laid aside,
And we must face each other
      and swallow that lump of pride,
And say and mean the words
      "I'm sorry and forgive me for my wrong",
Then, together with God's help,
      we can sing Salvation's song,
Why?! Because it's just
      the right thing to do.
You see, the sinners and backsliders
      are watching me and you,
And if they don't see the right example
      of what should be,
Then why should they want to be
      a Christian like you and me,
Together, we have a great responsibility
      to live right, come what may,
By truly having the love of God in our hearts
      each and every day!

GOOD MORNING LORD

Good morning Lord,
    You've given me another morning to see,
All the beauty of my little world
    You have given me.
Even if the sun don't rise
    I know my soul is free,
'Cause the Son has risen
    and my heart's on bended knee,
To thank You for always being
    where I need You to be.
So, my prayer of thanks is from the heart,
    that's the key.
So! Good morning Lord;
    just one more thing I want to say,
No matter what Satan does,
    I'm having a great day!!

HEAVEN OR HELL??!!

Heaven or Hell,
     which will you choose?
Heaven, you gain,
     Hell, you lose,
In Heaven, eternal life
     and heavenly glorification,
In Hell, endless pain
     and eternal damnation,
Again I say, Heaven or Hell,
     which will it be?
You are free to decide,
     BUT IT'S HEAVEN FOR ME!!

IN THE GAP

I'm standing in life's gap
     for my family,
'Cause I want them to go
     to Heaven with me,
I'm praying for God's hedge
     to surround them,
Keeping them safe,
     His Spirit drawing them to Him!!

HE DID IT ALL

He did it all
    for you and me,
He did it all
    that we could go free,
He left His throne
    to live as we on earth,
He came to a lowly manger
    for His birth.

He walked His journey
    according to His Father's will,
He bore the world's sin
    on Calvary's hill,
He willingly did for us
    what we could not do,
Yes, He did it all
    for me and for you.

He's preparing us a mansion
    with beauty beyond compare,
Yes, He's still doing it all
    because He cares,
You know, He's coming back
    some glorious day,
So, just look around,
    HE'S ON HIS WAY!!

BORN, WALKED, DIED, AROSE!!

He was born to become our Saviour one day,
He walked among us to teach us His way,
He died on the cross to forever cover our sin,
He arose to bring Salvation's Plan to all men.

He died on the old rugged cross to redeem us from our sin,
Only one sacrifice was needed; He won't have to die again,
He occupied the Manger, the Cross, the Tomb for you and for me,
But! He conquered all three just to make us free!!

THREE IN ONE IN THE SKIES

I saw some crosses in the blue, blue sky,
I said to myself, "Hey! My Oh My!"

Someone from somewhere is flying an airplane,
They must be a Christian flying in Jesus' name!

One trail was a few trails making one in my eyes,
Three separate trails crossed the one making
       THREE IN ONE IN THE SKIES!!

USE YOUR IMAGINATION

Just think of the pain that Jesus endured
   for all of us on that day,
Use your imagination and think how the nails
   pierced His skin as He lay,
Those nails were primitive and only
   a heavy hammer could make them go through,
Yes, the precious skin of our Saviour
   was pierced just for me and you.

Can you imagine the agonizing pain,
   yet, even then He loved you and me,
He felt so alone; even the Father turned away;
   sin He could not bear to see,
The sky grew black, He gave up the ghost and arose the third day
   just like He had said,
Yes! Praise His name, He died, He arose;
   all our sin debt is paid!

So, when you are feeling down,
   remember all He did for you and me,
Then, your spirit will be lifted, happy,
   and for sure it will be free!!

HEY! DEVIL!

Hey! Devil, no matter what you say or what you do,
One of these days is gonna be the end of you,
You go about causing trouble and sewing discord,
But, devil, you ain't no match for our Lord.
You jump from shoulder to shoulder telling lies,
One day you're going down to a pit never to rise,
'Cause our God has more power than you know about,
Yeah! We're leaving this old world with a shout!
So, we're giving you notice, no matter, we'll stand,
You're defeated already, we're going to Gloryland!
You're an evil, mean and aggravating kind of being,
You mean to steal our joy without our even seeing,
But, our ever present Comforter is leading us along,
With Him, we'll win this battle while singing
    OUR VICTORY SONG!!

Maxine Dykes Quinton

I FEEL A HUG COMING ON!

I feel a hug coming on,
  as I praise His name,
He's always close by,
  He's always the same,
When I need to be encouraged,
  He's always near,
He hugs me and says,
  "Take another step, never fear!"

HE MUST BE WHY!!

You've heard "My foot's on the Rock
  and my mind's made up";
Also, "If I but ask,
  He'll fill my cup".

Well, if we put our feet and our minds
  in the right place,
He'll help each and every day
  with His Mercy and Grace.

He can make all of us perfect
  in the twinkling of an eye,
But, we must do our part,
  making Him the only reason why!!

WATER UNDER THE BRIDGE

A whole lot of water has gone under the bridge;
      some muddy and some clear,
But, both for sure had an ever-present
      Help standing near.
Now, that muddy water;
      it broke my heart, but not my spirit,
'Cause even when we can't see the situation,
      clearly God is always near it.

He sometimes allows our water to be troubled,
      just so we can see,
What direction to take in order to be
      where we need to be.
Now that clear water represents
      the good and happy times of our lives,
Like family and friends and
      blessings when a child arrives.

Our Lord wants us to swim in clear water
      and not take a detour,
Any detour is our fault, so in taking it
      we learn to endure.
He tolerates our feeble minds when we are stubborn
      and make a wrong choice,
But He leads us along if we will follow
      and then we can rejoice.

We learn to lean on Him to take us
      through the muddy to the clear,
'Cause whatever troubled water we jump into,
      He is always near!!

OUTSIDE, INSIDE

Oh! My goodness! Bags under my eyes,
    crow's feet and wrinkles are so plain to see,
But on the inside, arthritis, bursitis and lumbago
    talk silently and directly to me,
All together, they tell me I'm getting old;
    that could make me sad and bring some tears,
But! I'm not crying; I'm rejoicing
    'cause my heart's in good shape; no fears,
In spite of aging signs, my heart,
    in His eyes, is in perfect condition;
So, I hope you will accept your age as a path to perfection
    as I read this rendition,
It's not what we look like on the outside
    but what He's done within,
Most important, the miracle at the Cross;
    Salvation from all sin!!

IN SPITE OF

In spite of negative words that are thrown my way,
I'm gonna keep on keeping on each and every day,
With God; I'm safe and secure come what may,
Yes! In spite of all, I'm gonna stay in The Way!!

NIP IT!!

If you have something you need to stop,
      Just nip it, nip it, nip it!
Ask Jesus to apply His blood and
      He will dip it, dip it, dip it!
Then you will be free
      if to Him you give it,
Free indeed!
      Then His way you can live it!

TEARS

Thank you Lord for tears
      of sadness and gladness,
For the tears that soften
      and start my heart,
For tears that fall down my cheek
      and being meek,
For tears that help me see
      and more humble be,
For tears for others;
      being my sisters and brothers,
Yes, thank you Lord for tears;
      helping my DEVOTIONS, EMOTIONS,
          MOTIONS AND NOTIONS!

WINGS OF THE WIND

You have felt but have you ever seen
    the wings of the wind?
To us they are invisible,
    but we can feel where they have been,
Their flutter is pleasant because He is flying
    and walking thereon as they go by,
Each time the wind blows, we know
    on wings of love He is drawing nigh!
Even if there is a great, great storm
    He is always, always there,
Just like in the storms of our lives,
    because He really, really does care,
So, when you feel a gentle or a fierce wind,
    just be very sure,
That He's right there with you
    and He will help you to endure!!

SHOUT!

Hey! Feed your faith
    And starve your doubt!
You'll be so happy,
    You'll just have to shout!!

NO DEBT

No bankruptcy or foreclosure filed in Heaven
    so don't you forget,
Everything there is paid in full
    there is absolutely no debt,
No mortgages, no liens or even dollars and cents
    to pass from hand to hand,
Yes! Everything will be perfect and debt free
    in that great land,
We just need to make daily deposits of praise
    each and every day of life,
Then we can live in that land
    that is free from all heartache and strife!

A HUMBLE PRAYER

Lord, give me boldness that's humble
    and humility that's bold,
Lord, I need these characteristics to do more;
    please don't withhold,
Help me step forward,
    knowing You will be by my side,
Yes, Lord, give me boldness and humility,
    let Your Spirit always abide.

Maxine Dykes Quinton

MIRROR, MIRROR

Mirror, mirror; can you tell me
      something about me?
Not my wrinkles, nor my gray hair
      But what on the inside I be?
Are the thoughts of my mind
      good and honest and true blue?
Do my eyes look only
      for the good things to do?
Does my mouth speak encouraging words
      to all that I meet?
Does my face have a smile
      for every person I greet?
Mirror, Mirror; when I look
      at my natural self as I abide,
Show me that Christ our Lord
      is living on the inside,
Please, don't let the things of this world
      fog up my reflection,
'Cause; by the Grace of God, I mean to be
      'caught up' in that FINAL RESURRECTION!!!

THE OTHER SIX DAYS

We attend church on Sunday;
      we fellowship, using all our Christian ways,
Then the rest of the week,
      what about the other six days?
Do we pray; read the Word,
      let our light shine and lend a helping hand?
Or, do we forget, let down our guard
      and fail to take our Christian stand?
When we walk down the street,
      do we have a smile and politely say "Hi"?
Or, do we purposely avoid someone,
      glance at them, and go right on by?

No, one day out of seven isn't much devotion
      to God and His loving ways,
We allow our carnal nature to cause us to fail;
      what about the other six days?
Each day, we need to ask God for His strength
      to face each new trial,
That can mean to wipe the frown off our face
      and go on with a smile,
And to use each situation
      to give God all the glory,
Because He is the author and shining star
      of this great story.

THIS MORNING

The birds woke me this morning
    with such a happy song,
They seemed to say, "Get up!
    you've been laying there too long!",
I turned over and looked outside,
    the sun was shining bright,
I felt thankful in my heart
    that God would show me such a beautiful sight,
After I got up, I looked outside again and said,
    "Thank you, Lord for the day,
But, most of all, I thank You, Lord
    for showing me the way,
To love everyone,
    even though with them I may not agree,
And for showing me the perfect plan,
    the plan of salvation that is free."

A PRAYER FOR COURAGE

Lord, I give You everything that I'm not,
Take what's left and make for You a lot,
Give me boldness and humility to stand up for You,
Take my shyness, give me courage to step and do.

A GREETING FROM GOD'S CREATION

For me, early morning
     is my time of the day,
All God's creation is waking
     and it seems to say,
"Good morning and welcome
     creation out of clay,
Here's another day for you,
     God will show you the way."

Listen as He speaks
     through a ray of glistening sun,
And through a rippling stream
     as it takes its run,
Listen all day long
     after your day has begun,
God speaks through all creation;
     His love compares with none.

PEACE LIKE A DOVE

Thank you Lord for doves you scatter along my way,
Your peace like a dove is with me each and every day,
I only have to seek it with my whole heart from you,
Then that heavenly peace will be with me in all that I do!

HOW TO BE HAPPY

Make sure every day
      that you walk in the Light,
And you won't have to worry
      about walking upright,
You see, that Light lights your way
      as you go along,
At the same time He will put
      within your heart a song,
And a smile on your face
      for everyone to see,
Then on the inside
      you'll be as happy as you can be!

HE KEEPS ON—SO SHOULD WE!

He keeps on keeping on loving and forgiving,
So we must keep on keeping on His Way a living,
'Cause, if we don't, we'll go down instead of up,
So, every day, love Him, asking Him to fill our cup,
If we walk upright before Him, He'll fill us to overflow,
Then there'll be no question to which place we'll go!

AN INVITATION

We're invited to a wedding,
      the invitation is signed and sealed,
We can attend this royal wedding
      if at the Cross we've been healed,
Christ has paid the cost of this wedding
      with His blood on Calvary,
He's preparing a marriage supper
      especially for you and me.

The dress code is very simple,
      it's purest white of the purest kind,
No spot or blemish will be allowed
      and our countenance must shine,
When He calls each of us by name,
      we must be ready his Word does say,
In the twinkling of an eye,
      in the midst of the air we'll be caught away.

So, are you ready for this wedding?
      Are you dressed in heavenly style?
If not, you can get ready,
      He'll go with you every mile,
As His Word says, "be ye also ready"
      He could come at any hour, (Matt 24)
Let's all be ready,
      all we need is HIS MIGHTY POWER!!

READ, READ, READ

What if someone took your copy
     of His Word away?
Could you remember enough
     to keep you each day?
God's Word will never be destroyed,
     that we know,
But no telling what will happen
     with Satan as foe,
He could cause an official
     to make a law of the land,
That the Bible be taken
     from every Christian's hand.

So we need to read
     and hide His Word in our hearts,
So we can just speak it
     to fend off Satan's darts,
If for some reason
     you can't read His Word,
Have someone read it to you,
     then you know it 'cause you've heard,
Then you can say "GET THEE BEHIND ME SATAN
     I'M GONNA LIVE GOD'S WAY,
I'VE GOT HIS WORD TO BACK ME UP,
     BUT ALL YOU'VE GOT IS DOOMSDAY!!"

WHO IS GOD?

Who is God, Who is God,
  Who is He to you?
Who lets the day awake
  and lets the sun shine thru?
Who lets the sun shine daily
  and the moon at night?
Who makes the grass so green
  and the flower's hue so bright?
Who provides food and all our needs
  each and every day?
Who gave His Son to free us from our sin
  and gave salvation's way?
Who sends spiritual sunshine into our lives
  and also the rain?
Who allows us to fall
  just so He can pick us up again?
Who strengthens us each day
  when we just simply ask?
Who has an abundant supply of love
  in which we can bask?
Who will lead us gently
  when we just hold onto His hand?
Who promised to take us safely through
  to Heaven's Gloryland?
Who is God,
  who is God above?
The answer to these questions lie
  in a simple word—LOVE!!

ME, MYSELF AND I

Is our attitude one of
        me, myself and I?
Or, is it concern for others
        and that Home on High?
Is our heart full of love
        and compassion for others?
Do we really care what happens
        to our sisters and brothers?
Are we seeking strength from Christ
        to be more like Him?
Are we lazy or
        are we full of vigor and vim?
Can we be touched
        to shed tears of concern?
In times of trouble,
        have we faith to stand firm?
Let's search our hearts
        and get rid of me, myself and I,
Put others in their place
        to gain that Heavenly Home on High!

VALLEYS

The valleys of our lives
      have a great purpose to help us grow,
Carnally speaking, a farm's bottom land
      has the richest soil we know,
Crops grow better there
      partly because of the water supply,
So, in our lives valleys draw us closer
      to that living water from on High,
So, let's not complain
      when a valley comes our way,
Let's just thank The Lord
      for all things every day!

WAKE UP

Wake up America!!
      You must turn your hearts in God's direction
Wake up Christian!!
      You must return to your first affection.
Wake up Dad and Mom!!
      You must use the rod of correction.
Wake up Mr. President!!
      You must do your part to stop this festering infection.
Wake up all people!!
      Let's strive together to His perfection!!

IN THE SHADOW OF THY WINGS

Lord, whatever problem comes my way,
　　help me hold on to You,
'Cause I know there's no one else
　　to take me through,
Grace and strength, Lord
　　for whatever You allow to come my way,
Your will be done,
　　may my heart and my mouth always say,
May I take refuge
　　in the shadow of thy awesome wings,
May I ask, seek and knock
　　until my heart sings,
For I know You are The Lord
　　of all people who ask,
And if I ask, seek and knock;
　　in Your love I can always bask!

SALTY OR BLAND?

Are we salty Christians
　　or have we lost our savor?
Are we bland not being seasoned
　　and in His favor?
Physical food needs seasonings
　　for it to taste it's very best,
We Christians need the seasoning of His Word
　　to stand the test!

WATCHING, WAITING, ANTICIPATING

Are we watching, waiting and anticipating
   His glorious return?
Yes, if we are walking in His Way
   and for others have concern,
But, watching is not just looking
   at the blue, blue sky,
It's the way we live each day
   knowing the day is nigh,
We've all got loved ones
   to whom we need to witness,
That important things of life are not just physical,
   but spiritual fitness,
Yes, as we joyfully await His coming
   after His spiritual church,
We know in Him we can find
   the peace and contentment for which we search.

GET ON OUTTA HERE, SATAN!!

Get on outta here, Satan,
   quit dancing on the avenues of my mind,
Get on outta here, Satan,
   as The Word says, "Get thee behind",
Because with God's help,
   I'm gonna stand for He's always near,
So, Satan, I'm giving you notice,
   "Get on outta here!!"

HOW'S YOUR ILLUMINATION?

Stars in the dark sky
      sparkle and give off light,
As we look, they appear
      like diamonds in the night,
You reckon God talks to the angels
      about our illumination?
You reckon He looks down
      and checks the brightness of our conversation?
Oh, He knows if we shine out
      or if under a bushel we hide,
Or if we use our spiritual power
      and in Him abide,
We need to make connection with Him
      for the power we need,
That power comes thru prayer
      and His Word if we let Him lead,
'Cause He's the main source,
      of this we can be sure,
We need to stay connected to that main line
      so we can endure,
So, if your connection has grown weak
      and your light is dim,
Just have your spiritual battery charged
      by re-connecting to Him,
Yes, He'll charge your battery
      and give a positive attitude to you,
Then, you'll have power to overcome
      any and everything Satan can do!

UNITY—LOVE IN A KNOT

No little groups or clichés
        in Heaven will there be,
For the redeemed will be equal
        in God's eye you see.

Unity will prevail in that City of Gold
        to worship our Lord,
In other words, in spirit and in truth—
        being in one mind and accord.

So, in preparation to go,
        we must be able to worship with other denominations,
Even if our views don't agree with theirs;
        love must be our demonstration.

We can't judge others
        if they don't worship the same way we do,
We don't want them to judge us;
        isn't that true?

Love is the strong cord
        that will bind us together,
Therefore, each of us must be willing
        to tie love's knot in sunny or stormy weather.

'Cause when He splits the Eastern sky;
        each will go up with the other,
So, let's extend our hand of Unity
        to every sister and brother!

OH!!!

Oh! I'm a longing to see my Saviour's face,
Oh! I'm a longing to finish life's race,
Oh! I'm a longing to go beyond The Milky White Way,
Oh! I'm a longing for that great and wonderful day,
Oh! I'm a longing deep within my soul,
Oh! I'm a longing to see that city of gold,
Oh! Are you a longing for the same as I am?
Oh! Let's all be ready to meet THE GREAT I AM!!

HUMBLE BOLDNESS AND BOLD HUMILITY

When there is a question of right or wrong,
    do we stand in boldness?
Or, do we go on unconcerned
    and just shrug it off in coldness?
You know, we don't need to be afraid
    to stand tall for the right,
'Cause if we make a sincere effort;
    God through us will shine bright,
When we have boldness—humbly displayed
    and bold humility brightly arrayed is a spirit that's ideal,
And if that spirit we possess—
    we will surely gain God's approval seal!

HANDS AND EYES

Lord, your hands of grace
    hold me safe each day,
Your eyes of mercy
    see my inner being and its way.

Your hands hold on tight
    so as I walk I won't fall,
Your eyes cause me to see
    you're the greatest of all.

So, Lord, use your hands
    and put me on your wheel,
Give me spiritual eyes
    to see you're really real.

Use my hands to reach out
    and help someone along,
Use my eyes to see their good points
    and not wrong.

Help my eyes and hands
    to encourage every day,
Put someone in my path
    to help along this way!!

31

HE LOVES US, EVEN THOUGH

Ever wonder what He wrote on the ground—
    I'd like to know,
Perhaps it was "I love you even though you do wrong,
    I love you even though, even though, even though,"
Ever wonder why He wrote the second time?—
    wouldn't you like to know?
Perhaps He was just repeating—
    "I love you even though you make mistakes—
    I love you even though, even though, even though."

Whatever He wrote,
    we just don't know,
But, what matters—He turned the accusers thoughts
    to themselves—so—they had to go, had to go, had to go,
His lesson to us is to look at our own faults
    before looking at others, this we all know,
So, if we have love for our sisters and brothers—
    that love we'll have to show, have to show, have to show.

Yes, whether His words are on the wall, on the ground
    or simply in His Book—they will surely turn the foe,
'Cause when Satan hears The Word—
    He has to go, has to go, has to go,
After all is said and done—
    whatever direction the winds of our lives blow,
He'll still mean the words—I LOVE YOU!
    EVEN THOUGH, EVEN THOUGH, EVEN THOUGH!!

FOCUS ON HIM

Let's keep our eyes
        clearly focused on our Lord,
Especially when we daily
        pick up His Sword.

Let's not allow Satan
        to get our attention in any way,
And if he does,
        we'll know just what to say.

Yes, when Satan temps us
        with his bag of tricks,
We can say "get thee hence,
        you're in for a fix.

You might as well lay off
        'cause we're on the winning side,
'Cause our Lord will never leave us—
        He will always abide.

So, let's adjust our focus button
        and keep our view clear,
Yes, with our eyes on Him—
        we will have no fear!

In the year of 1999, I visited my sister in Ohio. The following two poems were written on her back porch in the early morning:

SHARE HIS MORNING

Here I am on my sister's back porch
    facing the East,
On the beauty of a new day
    I can feast,
The sun is shining,
    the air is cool and crisp,
What a peaceful feeling
    to share God's morning like this.

There's a snowball bush
    and a small tulip patch,
The beauty of the morning;
    there's nothing that can match,
There's a field of green
    and a grove of trees to view,
Oh, what beauty God prepares
    for me and you.

Why, He prepares for us
    a special breakfast for the soul,
If we will only rise early
    and let our eyes behold,
Sometimes we take for granted
    a new day is on its way,
So, we need to rise early and with thanks
    share His new day!

RISE, BE STILL, LOOK AND LISTEN

From the same porch,
　　　　I see birds each a different kind,
For sure, God gives them an invitation
　　　　each morning to come and dine.

A robin red breast has come
　　　　for a breakfast that's free,
Other birds of many kinds
　　　　seem to say good morning to me.

Even a dove lights on the birdbath
　　　　for a cool morning drink,
I see a tiny brown and red bird,
　　　　could be related to the sparrow I think.

I'm waiting, hoping to see the squirrels
　　　　that live here by twos,
Must have missed their entry,
　　　　they're probably taking a morning snooze.

Now, I see a bunny rabbit,
　　　　hopping across the morning dew,
With its brown, fluffy fur coat on,
　　　　it greets the morning that is new.

The sun is shining brightly
　　　　and its light really does glisten,
We can see this beauty if we will rise early,
　　　　BE STILL, LOOK and LISTEN!

35

A MOTHER'S LOVE

Love is the main ingredient
      in the heart of a mother,
It's always there to be given
      like no other,
Whether we are right or wrong,
      we can depend on Mother's love,
For she has that extra something
      sent from above,
From tears to laughter,
      from scorn to praise,
Only God, Himself can understand
      a mother's ways,
Many virtues can describe
      a mother's beautiful love,
But the best example—
      having faith and trusting in God above!

A PRAYER FOR FORGIVENESS

Forgive me Lord for anything I've done that I shouldn't have,
Forgive me for anything I've not done that I should have,
My heart always wants to do right in Your sight,
Any failure is mine if I stray from Your light,
But, thank You Lord, that I can ask forgiveness at anytime,
May I always strive for good as this ladder to Heaven I climb!

HEAVEN

Won't it be wonderful to be up there?
No disagreements, no arguments; only His love to share,
Where is "there" you say; why it's that city of gold,
It's called Heaven; God's haven for our spirit and soul.

Christ is making it ready for us to share forevermore,
Yes, He'll lead us across that river to the other shore,
No darts to dodge and no words of scorn,
No darkness, only light and happiness on that morn.

We'll have a robe of white and a crown of gold,
Our countenance will shine as that city we behold,
We'll sing praises as He is crowned Lord and King,
Just think! Won't that be worth everything?!

Yes, everything we must go through to gain His perfection,
Oh! Let's always lift our eyes and hearts in that direction,
Yes, let's determine to go to that city on high,
Yes, let's look for our Lord to burst through that Eastern sky.

For He's coming soon to take us to that wonderful place,
Oh! Won't it be wonderful there to look upon His face?!
And to walk down that golden street and see our mansion fair,
Oh! I can hardly wait, I'm looking forward to being up there!!

SOMEDAY

Someday, I'm gonna have a new body,
    it will be glorified,
You see, this body is changing,
    this one in which I abide,
Age has brought me wrinkles
    and my hair has turned to silver,
But, one of these days He is coming back
    all of us to deliver,
From this evil world,
    He'll rapture us, taking us home,
And with my new glorified body
    I'll dance around His throne!!

A PRAYER IN JESUS' NAME

Lord, help me do the right thing
In every single thing,
Help me talk or sing
And may the praises ring.

And keep me safe and secure
Under your wing,
I know You can do it,
'Cause You're the Almighty King!!

In Jesus' name,
He's always the same!!

HE WILL PROVIDE

Perhaps we are overly concerned
       about having what we need,
But, does that concern include things
       considered to be greed?
God's Word tells us He will provide all
       if we walk upright,
So, if we do what He says,
       our future will be Oh! So bright!
Now, we may have to eat a little less
       and have fewer clothes in our closet,
But, any doubt that appears,
       that old serpent will certainly cause it,
So, let's hold on to faith,
       for He will always supply grace,
'Cause He knows we'll need plenty
       to run life's race!
Remember! He's Jehovah Jireh!!

HEAVEN

Heaven is a non-denominational place,
It takes a pure heart to win life's race,
A heart that is full of love,
Is what takes us to Heaven above,
So, it's not the building nor the sign over the door,
It's what's in our heart that makes us His forever more.

PEACH TREE TEA

Perhaps you don't know what I'm talking about
    when I say 'Peach Tree Tea',
Well, that's an old saying referring to a spanking
    for not being like you ought to be,
When I was a child, Peach Tree Tea was served
    quite often you see,
My Momma and Daddy didn't hesitate to serve it,
    even over their knee,
Why, sometimes boys and girls were served so much,
    you'd think they'd drown,
And sometimes they'd want to run away,
    but come mealtime they wanted to be found,
And, if it was served regular,
    you just couldn't help jumping up and down,
Perhaps, today, Peach Tree Tea
    has gone out of style,
But, you know, God serves us some
    once in a while,
We misbehave, step off the path
    and go mile after mile,
But, because He loves us,
    He chastises us and gives us a smile,
So, as we all go down the long,
    winding road of life,
Our lives can be happy, but along the way,
    there's sure to be some strife,
We might as well expect God to serve us
    His cup of Peach Tree Tea,
Because not one of us is perfect,
    But He still loves you and me!!

THANK GOD!!

Thank God for the empty cross
    and the empty tomb,
Thank God, Christ is alive
    and coming for us very soon.

Thank God, He's risen and is everywhere
    we need Him to be,
Thank God, we all were blind,
    but now we spiritually see.

Thank God, for His grace and mercy
    to me and to you,
Thank God, we can be Christ—like
    in all we say and all we do.

Thank God, we are new creatures,
    the old has passed away,
Thank God, we can all be ready,
    for He is coming, whether it be night or day.

Thank God, Easter is not bunnies, eggs, new hats, new dresses
    or even a new pair of shoes,
But, Easter is for Him, but in His wisdom;
    He gives us the choice and power to choose.

Thank God, He is the Resurrection and the Life
    and it's up to us to believe,
Thank God, it's up to us to accept and not reject,
    then Eternal Life we will receive!!

THANK GOD, HE LIVES!!

MATTHEW 7:1

When you look at your brothers and sisters,
      is it only their faults that you see?
But, when looking at yourself with all of yours,
      do you say "But that's me!"

Yes, when we look at ourselves,
      we tend to look only through a small keyhole,
But at others, we throw wide the door
      and criticize so cold.

So, let's take a mirror
      and look at our God given face,
And know that others, as well as us,
      are a part of this human race.

We shouldn't throw stones
      just because an act we don't approve,
We may be put in the same position,
      then it would be our move.

Yes, along the road of life,
      anyone's life can be smudged,
So, let's each remember and practice:
      JUDGE NOT THAT YE BE NOT JUDGED!!!

A PRAYER OF MINE

Lord, whatever is next,
    help me to stand up or kneel down,
Whatever is Your will,
    there let me be found.

You and I know,
    I want to do all things right,
We know the enemy
    is always there to fight.

So, strengthen me and give me courage
    to stand or kneel for Your ways,
Because standing or kneeling
    for the right always pays.

In Jesus' name, Amen

THE GREAT HEALER

He's the great healer,
    the great healer is He, only He can be,
He's always the great physician
    for you and me.

The doctors have wisdom,
    but they can only go so far, so far,
God himself gives them wisdom, but His healing touch
    is more able to bring you back to par.

WHAT'S OUR STRATEGY?!

When Satan comes at us,
  do we shake in our boots or our shoes?
Or do we keep our cool and walk on,
  it's up to us to choose.

We can back down or we can step up,
  which will we do?
We need to say "Satan,
  these boots are made for walking all over you!"

While we're walking; quote The Word
  while looking him in the eye,
'Cause The Word puts him on the road
  and he says, "bye-bye."

But he'll try again to set us up,
  to get us upset one more time,
So, let's just keep on quoting in Jesus name
  and say: "GET THEE BEHIND!!!"

TESTIFY!!

Have you been born again?
Have you been saved from sin?
Stand up, stand up!!
If you've ever been there, TESTIFY!!

Have you given your heart as a temple?
Have you claimed His promises so simple?
Stand up, stand up!!
If you've ever been there, TESTIFY!!

Have you been walking with Him each day?
Have you been talking, watching what you say?
Stand up, stand up!!
If you've ever been there, TESTIFY!!

Have you been watching that Eastern sky?
Have you been telling others why?
Stand up, stand up!!
If you've ever been there, TESTIFY!!

NOT MY WILL

Not my will, Lord but Thine be done,
Help me Lord, You are the only One,
On Whom for everything I can depend,
With You on my side, I'm sure to win,
The gift of love and the gift of Eternal Life,
Even though I meet with toil and strife,
So strengthen me Lord and make me strong,
Use me as You will and put within my heart a song.

Amen

JUST PEACE

No! Devil!
        You are not going to steal my peace,
So! Sneaky one!
        Your tricks might as well cease,
You're just a negative, tricky,
        conniving mean old beast,
'Cause I'm keeping my peace
        while on His word I feast,
So! Hear this! I speak!!
        PEACE! PEACE! PEACE!

ALWAYS BE CHRISTLIKE

SOME SPECIAL ABC'S:

Have . . . . AFFECTION	and not . . . . ANGER
Have . . . . BEAUTY	and not . . . . BITTERNESS
Have . . . . COMPASSION	and not . . . . COMPLAINTS
Have . . . . DEDICATION	and not . . . . DESTRUCTION
Have . . . . ENCOURAGEMENT	and not . . . . ENMITY(hostility)
Have . . . . FAITH	and not . . . . FURY
Have . . . . GLADNESS	and not . . . . GLOOM
Have . . . . HOLINESS	and not . . . . HATRED
Have . . . . INTEREST	and not . . . . IDLENESS
Have . . . . JOY	and not . . . . JEALOUSY
Have . . . . KINDNESS	and not . . . . KICK when down
Have . . . . LOVING SPIRIT	and not . . . . LUSTING
Have . . . . MERCY	and not . . . . MALICE
Have . . . . NOURISHMENT	and not . . . . NEGLECT
Have . . . . OFFER HELP	and not . . . . OFFENSIVE
Have . . . . PRAISE	and not . . . . PERSECUTION
Have . . . . QUIET SPIRIT	and not . . . . QUARRELSOME
Have . . . . RIGHT REPROOF	and not . . . . REVENGING
Have . . . . SANCTIFY self	and not . . . . SATISFY self
Have . . . . TOGETHERNESS	and not . . . . TRANGRESS
Have . . . . UNITY	and not . . . . Unfaithfulness
Have . . . . VERITY(truth)	and not . . . . Variance (discord)
Have . . . . WILLINGNESS	and not . . . . WITHDRAWAL
Have . . . . XAMINE(yourself)	and not . . . . XAMINE(others)
Have . . . . YIELD YOURSELF	and not . . . . YONDER at a distance
Be . . . . ZEALOUS	and not . . . . ZONKING OUT!!

ARTIST OF ALL ARTISTS

Lovely clouds of white and grays,
Against the sun's bright shining rays,
The sky beyond all shades of blue,
Such a beautiful site for me and you.

Yes, early each morning God paints it all new,
Each creation is shaded to just the right hue,
He is the Artist of all artists surely we know,
Never forgetting each day His love to show.

So, each morning when He allows us to open our eyes,
Let's not forget who He is, keeping our eyes on that Eastern Sky!

GONNA BE LEAVING

I'm gonna be leaving some wonderful day,
I'm going up past the Milky White Way,
When the trumpet sounds—all will know,
No—nothing can hold me when it's time to go,
No one knows the day nor the hour you see,
But He's coming back for you and me,
We must stay ready each and every day,
We know it's true—His Word does say!

JUST WHISPER HIS NAME

Don't need a prefix number
  or an operator to say, "Number please",
Just whisper His name from our hearts
  or while on our knees,
Don't need 'Old Ma Belle'
  or Bell South or even a dial tone,
Just whisper His name
  over our direct line to The Throne,
Don't need to worry if He will answer;
  don't even need a receiver,
Just whisper His name,
  His line always overrides the deceiver,
Don't need Apple, Blackberry,
  Road Runner or the popular Verizon,
Just whisper His name for His connection
  goes way beyond the horizon,
Don't need to go to www.com
  to get our 'voice' on The Line,
Just whisper His name,
  He always invites us to come on in and dine,
Don't need a computer, a regular phone
  or a phone called 'cell',
Just whisper His name
  on The Line that keeps us from Hell,
Don't ever get a statement
  at the end of the month to pay,
Just whisper His name,
  our 'Divine Connection' is paid in advance every day,
So! Let's just whisper His name
  to connect to that 'Divine Connection',
And, by the grace of God,
  we'll be with Him in that FINAL RESURRECTION!!

(This poem was written one week before my son, Steve, passed away.)

HIS INVISIBLE ARMS

Even before I knew I needed to be carried,
He carried me in invisible arms,
For twenty-eight years, He carried me lovingly,
And kept me from many harms.

Many times, being unaware of danger,
He was so very aware of me,
As I look back over the years,
All those times I can plainly see.

From twenty-eight years till now,
He's still carrying me each and every day,
You know what?! My faith tells me,
He'll carry me the rest of the way.

You know what else?! His arms are big enough
To carry all who call out His name,
'Cause yesterday, today and forever,
His love will always be the same!

A ROAD OF LIFE AD

There use to be an ad for greyhound bus that said:
"Ride our bus and leave the driving to us."
Well, I've got an ad for our Lord:
"Walk in His light that's not dim
and leave the shining to HIM!!"

TOO BUSY

Are we so busy, too busy,
For the things of the Lord today?
We eat, sleep, work and play then repeat,
We eat, sleep, work and play.

We have so much physical food,
We forget spiritual food for our soul,
To feast less and fast more,
Would make us more sincere and bold.

Rest is necessary but sometimes,
We're asleep even when we're awake,
Sleeping less and serving more,
We could throw Satan's blinders in the lake.

Work is right and necessary,
To maintain life's chain,
But to work less and worship more,
Is always heavenly gain.

Fun, fun, fun seems to be a reason to live,
For some people today,
But to play less and pray more
Can help many find The Way.

So, let's not be too busy to praise Him
As we walk life's highway,
We only need put Him first
Then we'll have plenty of time to eat, sleep, work and play.

THAT EMPTY SPOT

Do you have an empty spot inside
      that needs to be filled to the brim?
Do you know what it takes to fill it?
      Just fall on your knees in prayer to Him.

Yes, if you have a longing for satisfaction on the inside,
      just stop and think,
The only thing for your thirsty soul
      is a cup of living water to drink.

It doesn't need any additives
      to enhance the taste to perfection,
Just a drink of this 100% pure water
      will lead you in the right direction.

It's not just 99.99%, it's 100% living water
      that is sweet and pure,
And it will refresh you on life's journey
      and help you to endure.

I ask you again;
      do you have an empty spot on the inside?
Just open your heart to him
      and there He will abide.

R.S.V.P.

God is having a great homecoming,
        are you gonna take part?
No covered dish required,
        just a blood covered heart.

His word is your written invitation
        and you must R.S.V.P.
It's gonna be a great celebration
        and everything is free.

The dress code is simple,
        a blemish free robe of pure white,
The glory of God will be there
        and the Lamb will be the light.

Now, have you called for your reservation
        so you can take part?
If not, He still saves
        and applies blood to the heart.

R.S.V.P.—What will your answer be?

GOT YOUR TICKET?

Have you got your ticket to God's Gloryland?
It is covered by His blood—have you got it in your hand?
The fare is paid in full and there is no refund.
All that counts now is the race you choose to run.

Don't need to pack any bags to make the trip,
If your name's on the book, you're ready and well equipped,
So! Until departure time—just hold on tight,
'Cause very soon we're gonna take that heavenly flight!!

HARD OF HEARING?

Are we hard of hearing?
        Are our ears closed to His still small voice?
Carnally, we can lose our hearing;
        Spiritually, we don't have to unless it's our choice.

Quietness is necessary to hear Him speak,
        Even Christ sought quietness to hear his Father.
So, let's be quiet and still for His whisper,
        To Him it's no bother.

Carnally, we can get a hearing aide,
        To allow us to hear everything.
Spiritually, we just need to be still,
        And listen to our Heavenly King!!

MY LITTLE SPOT TO ENJOY

There's a little spot just
        outside my front door,
Early morning finds me
        sitting there once more.

The air is cool and fresh
        as I quietly look around,
I can feel His presence
        as I look up and not down.

Feeling His presence,
        I have the hope of eternal life,
For I know I can trust Him
        to lead through any strife.

Taking these few minutes of meditation,
        my day is off to a good start,
Along with a cup of coffee or tea,
        His presence stirs my heart.

Quietly, I thank Him
        for this another good day,
He made it just for me
        to enjoy along this way.

THREE SISTERS

These three sisters were talking,
      and here's some of what they said,
They all loved God and depended on Him,
      for whatever lay ahead.

Now, FAITH said,

      "My God is all powerful,
            on Him you can rely,
      Because He will walk with you,
            even when it's time to die.

      Sometimes, I'm so small,
            the size of a tiny mustard seed,
      But, if you are sincere,
            that's all of me you will need."

HOPE spoke up and said,

      "In Him lies,
            your highest expectation,
      Whatever you need is yours,
            if you give Him your dedication.

      When circumstances seem impossible,
            and all else seems to be gone,
      You can stand and say,
            Hope is alive and she's not alone."

Then, CHARITY had a lot to say,

    "You must love God,
        and every sister and brother,
    And I'll be wherever you need me,
        for God is love like no other.

    My cord is so strong,
        it will bind you together forever,
    And if you hold on tight,
        it can't be broken—no never."

Now, abideth—FAITH, HOPE and CHARITY,
    the greatest of these,
Being Charity, can only be attained,
    down on our knees.

These three must be used every day,
    in all that we do,
Now, these imaginary sisters,
    are just relaying a message to me and you!

DANIEL AND THE THREE BROTHERS

There was a man called Daniel,
With three spiritual brothers: Shadrach, Meshach and Abednego.
Now, Dan went into the lion's den
And he had no fear, you know.

For he knew God was on his side,
And he had no doubt,
He surprised these lions so much,
They said, "Well, shut my mouth."

"Why this man is so brave,
He just might give us indigestion,
We're used to people being full of fear
In this kind of congestion."

Dan talked to that pride,
And even put forth his hand,
He said, "You know my friend, Jesus?
He's the man who can!"

Those lions became so meek,
When they realized The Lamb was in the den,
They just rolled over like playful kittens,
And never opened their mouths again.

Now, Dan's three brothers,
They wouldn't bow to the King's idol god,
Even when he threatened,
To put them under the sod.

They told the King "Our God has power to rescue us,
But even if he don't,
We'll stand for Him,
To bow to your god—we absolutely won't."

So, into the fiery furnace,
Seven times hotter, they were thrown,
'Cause they loved their God,
The King's god they would not own.

The King had a great surprise,
He saw four men walking instead of three,
He said, "Look,
I just don't understand how it can be."

"Shadrach, Meshach and Abednego came out un-singed,
Just like they went in.
They were saved from the fire,
Just like Dan was from the den!"

The King's decree went out
To all the people in the land,
It said, "To worship the Only One True God,
The One Who can."

You know, these are only two examples
Of what God can do,
But, He's still working miracles,
Even today, for me and you.

Whatever situation we find ourselves in,
If we will just look up,
He's looking down, waiting for us,
To ask Him to fill our cup.

He really knows best,
What we need, you see,
Yes, He's still working miracles today,
For you and for me!

FIRE IN WATER

Floods, floods all over
      this great big world of mine and yours,
California, Florida, Baton Rouge
      and even on the New England shores.

There are fires in many places
      out of the control of man,
And so much evil and discord
      all over God's great land.

In various places the earth is belching up lava,
      killing as it flows,
Perhaps God is getting angry
      with this world such as it goes.

But, we as God's people know
      He can build a fire in the midst of water,
We and all things of this world
      are for sure in the hands of The Potter.

Yes, God is in control
      and He says destruction by fire this time around,
His Word tells us to be watching,
      for His fire and brimstone is soon coming down.

A GARMENT OF PRAYER

Put on your garment
     of prayer every day,
It will keep you warm
     and cozy in every way.

You will be stronger to face
     those darts that Satan throws,
And you can stand against evil
     as your faith grows.

May God put peace in your heart
     and joy in your soul,
May you hold on to God's hand
     knowing He is in complete control.

SMILE

SMILE!! You look better without a frown,
You see, a smile is a frown turned up-side down,
That's on the outside, but it works on the inside too,
If your spirit is joyful, your heart will smile, yes that's what it'll do,
Letting a smile be your umbrella protects you from the rains of life,
Yes!! We've gotta learn to smile even through toil and strife,
Because a better day is just around the bend,
He's coming to take us out of this world of sin,
When that trumpet sounds, we'll be on our way,
Just think!! The Last Day will be a Better Day!!

TEARS OF REMEMBERING

Lord, thank You for letting me
      be a Mom of four,
Thank You for the grace
      to be blessed even more.

To watch them all grow up
      thru the years,
And thank You for drops
      of 'Remembering Tears'.

Thank You for the
      strength to be
both Mom and Dad
      to a degree.

Thank You for inumberable blessings
      that You gave to us along the way,
And thank You for Motherhood,
      PRAISE YOUR NAME FOREVER IS ALL I CAN SAY!!

I'LL BE GLAD

I'll be glad when evil is gone,
I'll be glad when life is a song,
Glory, glory will be our praise,
What a glorious time in those days,
Where? Oh! Where will you go?
When we leave this world below?

A HUNTING I DID GO

From hunting long ago with my Dad
     to hunting with my son on an early morn,
All bundled up in twenty degree weather,
     I went hunting with my fourth born.

We walked down into the woods
     to a deer stand that looked like a tree-house,
We climbed into a space about six by nine feet,
     then sat there quiet as a mouse.

The sounds of the morning were all around us
     as we sat in the top of a tree,
With hilltops all around us,
     the light of the sun we could still see.

We waited and waited but saw no deer,
     but enjoyed the quietness of the morn,
So, this is a little story about going hunting
     with, Mark, my fourth born!!

V'S IN THE TREES

As this old lady sat in a deer stand,
      I could see V's in the trees,
On that cold, cold morning,
      the bare tree limbs formed lots of V's.

While bundled up in a comforter,
      my poetic mind wandered back over my life,
"V" stands for "Victory" and I've got victory
      over lots and lots of strife.

I didn't win by myself,
      I had help from my Heavenly Father above,
Some victories are harder to win,
      but He is all sufficient through His love.

So, if we will look around,
      we can see things to remind us of His grace,
He helps us win every day,
      if we only trust Him as we run life's race.

Those "V's" in the trees
      seemed to have eyes looking back at me,
Saying, "God has brought you a long way
      old lady, don't you see?!!"

DENOMINATIONAL AIR

The denominational air is foggy
      and needs to be clear,
Our hearts need to soften in a spiritual way
      and have no fear.

For God's 'spiritual church'
      will triumph in the end,
Yes, we need to be in unity
      to fight Satan's sin.

Christ makes the way to Heaven
      very, very clear,
There's no fog blocking our view,
      we can spiritually see from here.

He's sitting at the right hand of the Father
      awaiting His command,
"Son, go and bring my children
      out of that wearisome land."

People! It can't be long till we hear
      His mighty trumpet blow,
He's coming in clouds of glory
      to declare victory over his foe.

He'll take us home to live
      with Him forever more,
Yes! We'll each cross over
      to that beautiful shore.

And live with Him forever
      in that city of gold,
Won't that be a wonderful
      sight to behold?

We'll crown Him Lord of Lords
      and King of Kings on that day,
As we sing "Glory, Glory" to His name,
      and our burdens down we lay.

As we march around His throne,
      God's 'Spiritual Church' will be a mighty band,
There'll be no denominational parade,
      just a parade of true hearts in that land.

He will separate the good from the bad
      with judgment that is true,
Oh!! Aren't you glad He'll be the One
      to judge me and you??!!

RESCUE ME

I had a wreck,
I hit the deck,
I broke my neck
    —call the rescue squad!

I got in trouble,
My life is like rubble,
My burdens are double
    —call the rescuing God!

I took the wrong road,
I chose the wrong abode,
And heavy became my load
    —I called the rescuing God!

He's always on call,
Every time I fall,
He helps me stand tall
    —If! I call the rescuing God!

Hey! If your life is like pollution,
And you're seeking revolution,
He's the only solution
    —Bow and call the rescuing God!

So, next time your back is to the wall,
Remember to make that important call,
As in His Word; He'll change you from a 'Saul' to a 'Paul'
    —IF YOU CALL THE RESCUING GOD!!!

NO DENOMINATIONS IN HEAVEN

There'll be no denominations
       in Heaven for sure,
No earthly church name over the door,
       just hearts that are pure.

What counts is God's spiritual church,
       not one that is man-made,
For on The Rock is where
       it's foundation is laid.

We look at our brothers and sisters
       and gossip and scorn,
Why not give encouragement
       and show that we are spirit born.

If they have fallen,
       help lift them up and not down,
Yes, by helping instead of hindering,
       we'll all be Heaven bound!

I WATCHED THE CLOUDS THIS MORNING

I watched the clouds this morning
    as they moved on and on,
I saw cloud after cloud and then
    the clouds seemed to be gone.

Each cloud would take on a new form
    different than before,
Or was all the clouds really moving
    and being replaced by more?

I just sat there and watched
    and then the sky was clear,
I just wondered how it would be
    to be up there instead of here.

Some day we will all know
    when we lose our gravity,
And go through the clouds to live
    with our Lord throughout eternity.

And then I saw the light of the sun
    begin to rise in the East,
It began to give light to everything
    and whisper such sweet peace.

By now, God's creation was all visible
    and pleasing to the eye,
I thanked God in my heart for the now
    and also the sweet by and bye.

THE LONELY CLOUD AND THE SUN

There's a lonely little cloud
　　　　just floating in the sky,
Perhaps it's taking an angel
　　　　for a ride bringing it nigh.

To look things over down here
　　　　and maybe to wonder why,
So much turmoil has to be,
　　　　the angel lets out a sigh.

Here comes the sun—
　　　　it's playing peek-a-boo,
Saying, "I'm gonna shine today,
　　　　especially bright on you.

My Master has sent me
　　　　so you won't be blue,
I'm rising and shining
　　　　just to improve your view."

Now, the sun looks pink,
　　　　but just wait and see,
Soon, its hue will change to gold
　　　　for you and me.

The sun's playing peek—a—boo again,
　　　　it's behind a tree,
But, just like our God;
　　　　it's always there—that's the key.

YUM! YUM! FOOD! FOOD!

Food, Food, Food is shown
      every few minutes on TV,
I say it's another ploy of the devil
      to destroy you and me,
We need nourishment for our carnal being,
      but most eat way too much,
But we need to refrain from too much
      of fats, sweets, pop and such,
'Cause they are all harmful
      when we indulge in excess,
But spiritual food is always good for sure
      and that ain't no guess,
We have no problem digging into that juicy hamburger
      or that t—bone steak,
But, what about His Word;
      How much time do we make and take?
Time is well spent when we choose
      from the 'Free' buffet of God's Word,
'Cause with its nourishment,
      whatever comes along, He will undergird.

HEY!! THIS MORNING!!

From which side of the bed did we rise?
Was it the thankful side with happy eyes?
Or! Was it the grouchy side for me and you?
If so—we must take off the old and put on the new.

It's up to us—it's what we all must do,
Choosing to be happy and not blue,
To have a joyful day all day long,
The right side will help us have a song.

So—if we woke up grouchy we need to say a prayer,
"Lord, help me care what my face will wear,
Give me sweetness on the inside and a smile on my face,
And help me spread some cheer as I run this race."

DECEIT AND DEFEAT? NO!!
—FEAST ON PEACE? YES!!

Here comes deceit and defeat coming at me again,
Telling me I can't do anything about the put down pain,
But! I'm gonna put off that pain and put on peace,
And dine at God's table where there's always a feast!!

73

IF'S

If Christ had not been born flesh,
    where would you and I be?
We would be wandering around,
    blinded forever, you and me.

If He had not been the perfect example,
    how could we learn,
About His unconditional love and
    for our praise He does yearn.

If He had not gone to the cross and arose,
    just what about it?
We would have no joy of salvation
    and to the world couldn't shout it.

If He had not sent the Comforter,
    how could we make it from day to day?
We would have no power
    and could not at His feet our burdens lay.

If He hadn't ascended to the Father's right hand,
    how would we have prayer?
We would have no intercessor
    nor feel His spirit and know He's always there.

BUT! you see our Lord did all these things
    and so many more,
And by His great love we can live with Him
    forever on Heaven's bright shore!

AND'S

I'm positive that God loves me
AND understands me . . . AND God is real
AND God won't leave me . . . AND God forgives my shortcomings
AND God accepts me as His child
AND God lifts me up . . . AND not down
AND God speaks softly in my ear . . . AND God never yells at me
AND God saved me through my faith in Christ
AND God always supplies sufficient grace
AND God sent His Only Son as a baby to be my redeemer
AND God protects me 24-7-365-6
AND God loves me even though I'm not perfect
AND God sends blessings every day
AND God gives strength every day
AND God provides food for my table and shoes for my feet
AND God provides all my needs and some of my wants
AND God healed me of polio and depression
AND God helps me understand diabetes
AND God keeps my family safe from harm
AND God knows I walk upright so eventually
        my family will all serve Him
AND God has given me His Spirit to sustain me
AND God kept me from one abuse
        and brought me through another
AND God has a reason for everything
AND God is the past, the present and the future
AND God is King of Kings . . . AND Lord of Lords
AND God will send His Son back for me someday!
AND! The above are only a few among many blessings
        that God does for me and you.
But we need to be positive . . . AND keep our eyes on the prize
        at the end of this physical life.
We also must give God our praise
AND honor Him in all things.

BUT'S

Sometimes we may feel no one loves us,
      BUT GOD loves no matter what!
Maybe someone abandoned us,
      BUT GOD is the best friend we've got!
Some people only put us down,
      BUT GOD always lifts us up!
Every day we have needs,
      BUT GOD always fills our cup!

Perhaps we've been struck down with a sickness
      that seems beyond control!
BUT GOD touches the situation,
      heals making us feel whole!
One day we were all sinners
      about to lose our soul!
BUT GOD sent His Son and saved us
      making Heaven our goal!

Maybe we have a small abode,
      but we accept it with a smile!
BUT GOD has a mansion for us
      decorated in Heavenly style!
Sometimes life brings things to us
      that we don't understand!
BUT GOD will make all things new
      when we hold onto His hand!!

No matter what comes our way,
      let's remember the words:
        "BUT GOD!!"

ENCOURAGEMENT

HEY! Do you remember those trials
      He brought you through?!
HEY! Do you remember all those blessings
      He poured out on you?!

HEY! Sometimes just to look back and remember all the times
      He was by your side!!
HEY! Just to remember when you were drowning,
      He rolled back the tide!!

HEY! But to look forward to that city
      while to His hand we hold!!
HEY! Won't it be wonderful when we enter
      that city of pure gold?!

SHAKE TO WAKE

When a person is asleep and we need to wake them,
      Don't we shake them?
Don't you think God is trying to wake us
      With a shake to turn to Him?

WORDS FROM GRANNY AND GRANDMA

Granny would say "I love you,
Get your life in order and make it snappy,
'Cause when you do,
You'll be so peaceful and so very happy."

Grandma would also say, "I love you",
Then she'd say, "Walk upright before God all the way",
Your Granny and I are waiting
To see all of you some sweet day.

Some of you we didn't get to meet,
Looking forward to seeing all real soon,
So, look to Him for all your needs,
And be ready morning, night or noon.

'Cause He's getting ready to come for His own,
And bring them on home,
Please! Be in one accord as a family,
And not be left behind and all alone!

JUST ACCEPT

Can't change what comes our way,
Just accept it and go about each day,
God has purpose for everything He allows,
And has sufficient grace that He endows.

BEWARE OF THAT ROARING LION

Beware of that roaring lion
    as he walks to devour,
He has a sly, sneaking way
    to pounce at any hour,
He plays a crooked game
    so as to cheat us of our soul,
And take everything worthwhile
    with his crooked roll.

But, thank God, we have the power
    to win life's game,
"Get thee behind me Satan"
    still means exactly the same,
Thru Jesus Christ, our Lord,
    we have the power to resist wrong,
So, it's up to us to take a stand
    and sing salvation's song.

F.D.I.C.

Federal   Forever
Deposit   Deposited
Insurance   In
Corporation   Christ

I'm a millionaire
    and don't have much Do-Re-Me,
I'm still a millionaire in spirit,
    my soul is free,
My account records my activities
    each and every day,
Being my deposits of praise and prayer
    and blessing withdrawals all along the way,
No statements or checks required,
    my account is never in the red,
No FDIC needed 'cause the cross
    insures my account as daily I'm led!

MY HEAVENLY F.D.I.C.

He is my surety,
I'm safe in His F.D.I.C.,
My account always has a balance I can use
Whatever I ask in His name, He don't refuse
So, every day I must make a deposit of praise
Then my account will have a balance I can use all of my days!

THE SON / SUN

If you have 'clouds' surrounding you any given day,
Just look up, the Son/sun will melt those 'clouds' away,
Spiritually speaking, the Son is full of the warmth of God's love,
Behind carnal 'clouds' the sun's warmth is peace from above,
So, don't worry about the clouds of life, just look up,
Our Lord will take care of them and fill your cup!

I'M ONLY ONE PERSON

I'm only one person
    and you're also just one,
But with the trinity
    God's will can get done,
Now, I must not judge you
    and you must not judge me,
'Cause God judges both
    from his position of three,
He knows my heart
    and He knows yours too,
He really knows
    if we are a true blue,
So, let's each do
    our God given chore,
Then we'll see our name
    on our mansion door!

ROYAL SUPPER

We are invited to a royal supper
    so I am told,
We have an invitation
    engraved in purest gold,
We don't have to RSVP
    if we're already born again,
For his blood has made us
    free from all sin,
This royal supper will be
    perfect in every way,
For it will be spread
    with His love on that day,
Our Saviour will be there
    and He will serve us well,
What a time we will have
    as the old, old story we tell.

BEAUTY OF SPRING

As I see all the different flowers, etc.
    coming to life today,
I think how beautiful spring is;
    what more can I say?
Only God can sprinkle the seeds
    in just the right place,
All things become beautiful
    when touched by God's grace!!

YOUR WANT TO

Got some things you do
      that you know not to do?
Well, get in touch with Jesus,
      He'll change your 'WANT TO',
If you'll be sincere in your head
      and do your part,
Then He'll change your 'WANT TO',
      and also your heart,
If 'HE TEN' and 'THE BEES'
      are your pattern each and every day,
Just abide by 'THE TEN',
      and your 'WANT TO' will outdo wrongs along the way!

LOOKING AND SEEING

As we look across God's fields of green,
And think of all the beauty we've seen,
And if we could block out all man made things,
And see only what God made—what sweet peace it brings,
If we will just take time to look all around,
And if we're blue—this beauty will lift us up and not down!

THE OLD FASHIONED LAMP

Have we trimmed our 'wicks' lately to shine His light,
      Or are they crusty with sin?
Just as a 'wick' of a coal lamp needs trimming,
      To not blacken the globe within,
We must trim the crust of our life,
      Cleaning where the crust has been.

And does our 'chimney' need washing
      Clean and shiny for the light to shine thru,
Yes, sometimes our spiritual chimney gets black with 'soot',
      In spite of all we can do,
So, by allowing Him to wash us clean,
      Our chimney will shine like brand new.

But, for a 'wick' and a 'chimney',
      Of a coal oil lamp to lighten a space,
There has to be some 'fuel' in a container,
      Namely the lamp's base,
That 'fuel', 'The Three in One',
      Must be present for us to win life's race!

We are to be 'The Lamp' so to speak,
      And we must be right with God above,
Our heart and soul depicting the 'wick' and 'chimney',
      Must be fueled by His love,
Then our 'light' will shine brightly,
      And we'll be as happy and peaceful as a dove!

FLYING HOME AT LAST

On that 'great' day, there'll be no delays,
      And for sure no re-routing,
And there'll be no questions,
      No unbelief and no more doubting,
When it's time for 'flying',
      There'll not even be any time for shouting.

For our memory will be gone,
      Concerning the many trials of the past,
'Cause, in the twinkling of an eye,
      We'll 'fly' to meet our Saviour, faster than fast,
What a wonderful day;
      We'll be praising and shouting "Home at Last!"

Yes, people, that 'great' day is on its way,
      It is so very nigh,
We don't have time to fight each other,
      Or fret and fuss and question why?
So, let's get and stay ready to go,
      To our Heavenly Home via that Eastern Sky!

THOUGH HE SLAY ME!

Old Job was a rich man who honored God,
     And eschewed evil in all he did and said,
'Friends' accused and abused him,
     Till he kind of wished he was dead.

Wishing to never been born,
     Is really wishing you had never known life,
But, Job trusted God,
     Knowing He would take him through any strife.

Now, his wife was being a help meet,
     But in the wrong way for sure.
Telling him to curse God and die,
     But Job knew with God, he could endure.

So, through it all, Job trusted God,
     To take him victoriously all the way,
God repaid Job double for his trouble,
     And He will do the same for us today!

So, if you are being tormented by 'miserable comforters',
     Just keep on trusting God every day,
Then, whatever befalls you,
     Victory will be yours to defeat Satan and stay in The Way!

THE ALTAR

The altar is not a talebearer or a gossip,
    It tells not prayers from your heart,
Whether by your bedside, in the church,
    Or anywhere you might draw apart.

The altar is a place of honor and humility,
    That connects you directly to the throne,
Where you can talk secretly to our heavenly Father,
    To Him and Him alone.

Prayer works best when praises and thank you's are included,
    There's no doubt,
And when the answer comes,
    Your cup overflows and you just have to shout.

Sometimes we must wait,
    But we know His time and will is the best,
The answer could be no, maybe, or wait,
    But Oh! What joy when it's yes!

But, oh! If the altar could talk,
    What tales it could surely tell,
Thank God it don't, for the gossips and talebearers
    Would wear their jaws out! Well! Well!

LOOKING FOR A ROLE MODEL?

Jesus Christ is simple, yet Supreme, not complicated at all,
If you want the best role model, just answer the Lords' call,
He really wants to help you, on your journey of life,
He'll give you peace within, even when there is toil and strife,
He'll mend your 'achy breaky heart' and fill it with love,
Love for Him, love for others; yes, love from above.

Don't allow Satan to possess your thinking,
'Cause he will laugh as you are slowly sinking,
Into a web of drugs, alcohol, and intimate affairs,
He wants to keep you from serving Christ, the One who cares,
But, if you have God's power, you can tell him "get thee hence",
Then he'll flee and his threats won't be worth two cents.

Most of the 'role model' singers and stars of today,
Are just singing and acting to get the money you pay,
To hear their self-glorifying talents they display,
Some of the words are even reversed to lead you the wrong way,
They may try to deceive you; in other words, feed you a lie,
Then get you hooked to their ways and make you wonder why.

So, why not look to the 'ROLE MODEL' of all time,
Jesus Christ is the very best you can find,
Read and study about Him in Matthew, Mark, Luke, and John,
He'll give you the 'NEW BIRTH'; He doesn't need a magic wand,
He comes into your heart and changes your whole attitude,
You'll have strength you never dreamed,
     IF! In your life, CHRIST YOU INCLUDE!

AMERICA!! BLESS GOD AGAIN!!

America, let's bless God again,
   turn from evil now and repent,
If we want more and more blessings
   to be Heaven sent.

We seem to have forgotten
   just how we started long ago,
Our founding fathers used God's way
   as a pattern, don't you know.

If we as a nation refuse to obey His way
   and refuse to be humble,
Then we as a nation will surely do more
   than carelessly stumble.

We'll fall into Satan's trap
   and become a nation in defeat,
But!! To be 'Under God' again,
   we just can't be beat!!

So! Let's each one stand
   and hold God's banner way up high,
Yes!! Let's stay ready
   and keep our eyes on that eastern sky!!

SUNRISES AND SUNSETS

Praise and thanks to our Lord
      for each sunrise and sunset,
Each reflection across the sky,
      how much more beautiful could it get?

If you've never watched a sunrise,
      you've missed a beautiful sight,
If you've never watched a sunset,
      you've missed beauty before the night.

Each of our lives, so to speak, starts with a sunrise,
      our first breath of life,
And ends with a sunset,
      our last breath to end all our strife.

There's been so many earthly sunrises and sunsets
      for all of us to see,
But, the lives we live in between
      determine where our eternity will be!

On earth, we enjoy the rising
      and the setting of the sun,
But, just think, when in Heaven,
      we see face to face The Son.

We have 'JOY' on earth with God's creations
      as we live life's story,
But, in Heaven, 'JOY UNSPEAKABLE'
      at His feet, sharing His glory!!

JUST WANNA BE A BLESSING

Just wanna be a blessing
      as I travel this gospel road,
Just wanna be a blessing
      and help someone carry their heavy load.

Just wanna be a blessing
      with my heart full of song,
Just wanna be a blessing
      till the Rapture; can't be very long.

So, Lord, every day give me something to say
      and something to do,
That will show that I love,
      honor and glorify YOU!!

GIVE UP!! GIVE UP!! NO WAY!!

You've heard the saying: "I'll just give up,
      I'll just throw up my hands and quit,"
Well, God's people can't do that,
      'cause we'll end up in that awful pit.

We must keep on keeping on
      living His way every day,
Then our hands will go up in victory
      as our burdens upon Him we lay!!

TEARS OF CONCERN

Lord, don't let me cry tears of pity
      and despair for poor little me,
Only let me cry tears of concern
      and burden for my family.

Surround each one of them
      with your hedge of protection,
Shake the ones who need to be shaken
      to salvation.

May I speak when needed
      and be a good example at all times,
May I project your love to each one;
      the tie that binds.

Praise your name for my family,
      each being special in their own way,
Lord, I love you and I love them
      through my tears is all I can say!!!

THE GREAT CREATOR

I'm acquainted with
    the Great Creator of this world,
He's always available to hear
    the words of His little girl.

He never betrays me
    and He's always close by my side,
He provides my every need
    as in His way I abide.

Oh! I'm acquainted with
    the Great Creator of this world,
He's leading me all the way
    to those gates of pearl!!

HONOR AND HELP

I always want to honor Him
    and help someone at the same time,
Whether words of simple truth
    or a bunch of good words that rhyme.

So, as you listen to the words
    I am reading to you,
I want to honor Him,
    and help and encourage you in all that you do!!

THE THREE

To God, the number "three"
      was important His will to fulfill,
There were "three" nails, "three" words, "three" days
      and "three" crosses on Golgotha's hill.

"Three" nails held the carnal body
      of our Saviour there,
"Three" words were spoken by our Saviour
      as He hung there, our sins to bear.

But!!! "Three" days later He didn't stay there!
      He arose and He came out!
The fact is that the word "Trinity"
      covers it all, is what it's all about.

That word "Trinity" means "Three",
      The Father, The Son and The Holy Spirit!!
So, every day, let's trust 'The Trinity'
      of the cross and stay ever near it!!!

SMILING THROUGH MY WRINKLES

Lord, help me smile
      through the wrinkles on my face,
May my insides be smooth as silk
      and beautiful as lace.

Even though the wrinkles just hang around,
      help my eyes look up to you,
For You are all I need to be strong
      and make it all the way through.

Thank You Lord for always
      being there just for me,
May I walk each day in Your way
      that makes me forever free.

Thank You again
      for being there
'Cause I know
      You really do care!!

DANIEL AND THE LIONS

Just imagine old Daniel
  in the lion's den,
As his heavenly Father
  came to defend.

Daniel said "Here Kitty, Kitty,
  I need a pillow for my head,"
So, that old lion just rolled over
  and did what Daniel said.

There he lay asleep
  with the other lions lying all around,
As he slept, those lions didn't growl
  or even make a sound.

When he woke up, he said,
  "Good morning" to that pride,
Daniel knew all the time
  that his heavenly Father would abide!!

DOVES FROM GOD

Two mornings in a row,
      I saw two doves in the morning air,
The first morning, right in front of my windshield,
      flew up one pair.

They seemed to be there
      just for me to see,
Oh what morning beauty
      God can create just for me!!

REVIVED

Let's be revived by storing
      His word in our hearts,
Then we'll be ready to fend off
      old slewfoot's darts.

If we know His word,
      then we won't be deceived by a lie,
We can throw those darts right back at Satan
      when he draws nigh.

So—let's read, study and store
      His word each and every day,
Then we'll be worthy soldiers
      in this Army of the Lord all along the way!

GOD'S SIGNATURE

God's signature is on His creations
      both day and night,
Sometimes we might wonder whether he writes
      with His left or right.

But it makes no difference
      whichever it may be,
His signature is so evident
      for all of us to see.

His signature is written each day
      on the sun shining bright,
And all across the starry sky
      each night.

Even on the blowing wind
      and on the falling rain,
He writes us a message each day;
      He loves us all the same!!

MOTHER

What does Mother mean to me?
    What does Mother mean to you?
Her love is next to God's love—
    It's always true!

If we are Mothers,
    That's a great blessing from above,
'Cause God sent children,
    To fill our lives with love.

Sometimes they're good,
    And sometimes they're bad,
But we love them anyway,
    Whether lass or lad.

So, being a mother
    Is a great blessing from above,
The only love that's greater 'Mom's' love
    Is God's love.

So, the best inheritance we mothers can leave our children
    Is the knowledge of right and wrong,
Then, as they remember us,
    That memory will fill their hearts with song!

I'm so thankful to be a Mother. I have been truly blessed with four children, eight grand children and one great grandchild. I pray that all of them will put God first in their life. Then we can all be together in heaven some sweet day! I pray that God will help me to live in such a manner that they will see Jesus in me! Thank God for Motherhood!!

HIS HANDS

He's reaching out His hands saying,
    "Give me all your burdens and cares,"
He's reaching out his hands
    For all our troubles He really shares.

Oh! If we would only give
    All our concerns to him,
He loves us so much
    That He will always take care of them.

His hands are big enough to provide
    Every need that we have here below,
And He will always reach down and protect us
    From that ever—present foe.

Yes, He'll fight that foe
    For us no matter what,
If we trust Him to be
    The best friend we've got!

COOL, CALM AND COLLECTED

COOL . . . .
    'cause I'm following the golden RULE,
CALM . . . .
    'cause I'm resting in His hand—right in the PALM,
COLLECTED . . . .
    'cause He always loves me—I'm never REJECTED!

I'D LIKE TO GO SOMEWHERE

I'd like to go somewhere,
  Where there's peace and quiet.
I'd like to go somewhere,
  Where there's no wrong, only right.

The only place I know,
  Is a place called Heaven above;
For it's to be filled,
  With peace and joy and love.

WASTE?

Is your life overflowing with dung?
  Today or at any time?
One definition of dung is waste,
  That's not worth even a dime.

We waste money and gas going nowhere,
  But how much time do we waste?
Do we use time wisely walking upright?
  Or just running around in haste?

People! We don't need to waste any time,
  'Cause time is passing fast!
We must stay busy with the important things of God,
  They're all that will last!

BIRD'S EYE VIEW

How'd you like to be like birds,
      And have a bird's eye view?
God gave birds good eyes on purpose,
      To see from way up in the blue.

Morning time when I put out birdseed,
      Most of the time, no birds in sight,
But pretty soon there they come,
      God's creation—birds in flight.

We're not meant to have a bird's eye view
      Of that heavenly home above,
But, with spiritual eyes we believe,
      And trust that it's there, filled with love.

So, we don't need a bird's eye view
      To see what we need to see,
Just spiritual eyesight to trust God in His wisdom
      To take care of you and me!

FROWN OR SMILE?

I'm not going down with a frown!
I'm going all the while with a smile!

'Cause I've got so much to smile about!
Not gonna set around and pout!

Yep! While I'm doing my part!
His great love fills my heart!

Nope! Not going down with a frown!
Yep! Going all the while with a GREAT . . . BIG . . . SMILE!!

A LOVE LETTER

Carnally, a love letter is a written letter to someone
        that is precious to the writer
        telling them they are so sweet.
Spiritually, The Love Letter from our Lord
        telling us how precious we are to Him
        is so neat and just can't be beat.
His letter is full of promise and blessings
        that He bestows upon us
        each and every day.
Every page of His Word has the word 'LOVE'
        written in red
        telling of His Way.

EACH DAY

Let's put on a garment of humility
      each day as we rise,
Running life's race;
      keeping our eyes focused on the prize.

Yes, by keeping on keeping on,
      we can all win this race,
And someday thru all these trials,
      look upon His face.

He'll say, "Well done my child;
      you've kept the faith for so long,
Now enter into my heavenly choir
      and sing victory's song."

So, each day let's also
      send up a shout of praise,
Because after all,
      that's where our treasure lays!

OLD OR YOUNG—STILL APPLIES

Let's all us old people talk
    About our aches and pains,
But with faith in God,
    That on the throne He reigns.

We're old enough to know
    He will ease our aches and pains.
When we look to Him for strength,
    We have no losses, only gains.

Our faith and trust in Him
    Eases our hurts each and every day.
He will not forsake us in our old age,
    Come what may.

So, if you admit to being old or young
    Just put your trust in Him today,
And keep your eyes on that eastern sky
    And stay in 'The Way'!!

YOU LIGHT UP MY LIFE

You light up my life
    and give me courage to go on,
You light up my life
    and fill my heart with song,
You light up my life
    walking with me every day,
You light up my life
    giving me strength along the way.

Oh! How blessed I am
    that you light up my life,
Yes! You bless me, carrying me
    through much strife,
Oh yes! You light up my life
    as I'm growing old,
You'll keep lighting up my life
    on my way to that city of gold!!

HE KNOWS

He knows where
      we're supposed to be,
He knows everything
      about us, you and me.

He knows our hearts
      and what's on the inside,
He knows its desires
      and will lovingly provide.

He knows where
      we should be in our life,
He knows all the hurts,
      disappointments and strife.

He knows just how to solve
      each problem on life's narrow road,
Yes! He knows where we are,
      so let's let him carry our load!!

IF YOU WERE A STAR

If you were a star, could Jesus be found
      If someone followed you today?
Does your light shine bright enough
      That they wouldn't lose their way?

Do you have a countenance that reflects Him
      When others look upon your face?
Do your feet walk a straight path
      As you run your daily race?

Do you give out rays of love so strong
      That they would have no doubt?
Would your radiance be so bright
      They would know what Jesus is all about?

The Star of Bethlehem shone brightly
      On that night of so long ago,
So, let's shine for Him in such a way
      That others are sure to know.

That He's no longer in a manger or a grave,
      But via the cross He lives in your heart,
And if they will kneel at the cross,
      He will save them and do more than His part.

Oh! We could become a star on TV,
      In the movies or in the music world,
But! Let's become a shining star for Jesus Christ,
      Helping His name to be forever heralded!!

THAT TRICKY OLD DEVIL

That tricky old devil;
Watch out for him; He gets around,
He don't care what evil he does,
Just so he gets you hell—bound.

You know, he sits on someone's shoulder
And whispers his lies about you;
Then he jumps over to your shoulder
And lies to you too.

Then on down the road
He goes to cause some more trouble,
If he can, he'll take a person's good works
And turn them into rubble.

Don't underestimate him;
He's a fox that's cunning and sly,
He'll trick you when you least expect it
And make you wonder why.

But if we will depend on God
To lead us every day,
We'll be conscious and alert
When Satan gets in our way.

The words 'Get thee behind me'
Will be our spoken defense,
Then Satan's tricks of evil
Won't be worth two cents.

CAST THE FIRST STONE

You know, words of scorn can hurt and injure a person,
     Worse than a slap in the face.
Yes, we all have made mistakes at one time or another;
     We, as members of this human race.

We should be careful what we say,
     Even if the rumor about a person could be true;
Because, we may have to eat those words,
     Whether they be many or few.

We should let gossip stop with us
     And not spread hurtful words of scorn;
Really, we should just simply keep our mouth shut
     And show we are spirit born.

So, if you feel you must say words that hurt,
     In person or on the phone;
Just stop and remember; Christ said,
     "He that is without sin; cast the first stone."

JEHOVAH JIREH

Oh! Only a few years ago
      when I was but a teenager,
I was broke and had I wanted to,
      I had no cash to wager,
But, along came a few little children
      and I became a babysitter,
At 35 cents an hour, I became 'rich'
      and just couldn't be a quitter.

Why! That 35 cents would buy me seven ice cream cones;
      to quit? I wasn't dumb,
It would also buy seven bottles of pop, seven candy bars
      or 35 wads of bubble gum,
Well, it wasn't long 'til I was making 50 cents;
      I was on cloud nine,
With all that dough coming in, I could say,
      "I earned it, it's mine".

At the same time, I pin-curled
      a neighbor lady's hair so red,
Another neighbor had me do weekly cleaning,
      "I'm getting even richer," I said.
At age 16, I worked part—time at the five and dime
      'til I graduated from high school.
Then full—time; but a better job came, a telephone operator
      —Oh, how cool!

Since I was making so much; with my first check,
      I just had to shop,
With that check, I bought my heart's desire;
      a Brownie Hawkeye, I was on top,
During the next eighteen months,
      I met a 'guy' and oh! My! I was in love!
In a few months, I jumped the broomstick;
      I thought it was from heaven above.

Public jobs ended for work in a family business
       where I became a flunky,
Cook, waitress, bookkeeper and
       becoming a mother of a son, I got a little chunky,
That was the start of the blessings of my four children
       —real live doll babies,
They were truly blessings from God;
       no 'ifs', 'ands', 'buts' or 'maybes'.

Years passed, as ten years got close;
       God revealed to me that my 'guy' was untrue,
It was then I trusted God as Saviour saying,
       "Lord, I'll depend on You."
Without going into details,
       God gave me grace to go the extra mile,
Divorce came to our home, but through it all,
       God was there all the while.

My children, ages two through nine,
       didn't understand save one,
He flip flopped on the couch and started crying,
       my first born son,
Momma held out her arms and said,
       "God will take care of us if we let Him."
Even though my faith was strong,
       the future seemed kinda dim.

But it is darkest before the dawn,
       in every situation that we face,
God in His mercy always
       has a sufficient supply of grace.
He supplied a babysitter, my momma,
       came to live with us to help out,
She truly was a blessing to all of us,
       there was no doubt.

Then God opened up some jobs for this momma
     to help raise this family of four,
A political office job lasted ten years, but I decided to change;
     God opened another door,
My family didn't know about my fleece before the Lord
     nor did anyone know,
But when you trust God for whatever,
     He'll fight for you no matter the foe.

Another job as a bank teller came at less money, but benefits;
     I knew I should change,
So, you see, when we need to be in another place,
     God can really re-arrange,
Then, failing once more to make love work,
     I re-entered the work force,
Words came to me "you won't be able to get a job",
     But! I had a heavenly source.

Since then, I've had another office job for five years,
     but got an early retire,
'Cause that 'guy' of years ago, he retired from life,
     it was his time to expire,
For me to retire early, certain conditions had to be met;
     they were and I was glad,
You see, God and Uncle Sam had a retirement plan for Maxine
     she didn't know she had.

After two years of sitting at night privately
     that started during the five year hospital office job,
I wasn't in need but just wanted to be busy
     and not sit around and sob,
So! What do you suppose?! Another job showed itself
     in a flyer at the post office desk,
Now, this time, Maxine really had not made
     a formal job request.

Hey! This volunteer job pays less than regular pay,
  but the money is free,
No tax and not counted against my rent, etc.;
  hence God's blessings on me,
Recently, within my group, two jobs
  have become available from Him to me,
As of January 2009, I will start another office job
  with twice the money and it's still free!

By now, you've gathered that this poem is about provision
  for my family and for me,
But, even in times like we're facing, He'll do the same for us,
  our Provider He will always be!
My job now is rewarding as I am exposed
  to more people than before,
At first I questioned myself for changing jobs,
  but God knows just when to open another door.

Before I basically had only three plus people
  to encourage each place I would be,
But now I have fifteen plus to account for
  and encourage don't you see,
In His wisdom God always has a better plan
  than we can ever know,
And I know He has a plan for the rest of my life
  as each day I go!!

   PRAISE GOD!! JEHOVAH JIREH!!

A TEAR

God must have shed a tear
      For all that had to be.
We know He gave His only son
      To die on Calvary.

God must have shed a tear
      To see His son in agony,
But it was the only way
      To redeem you and me.

Sometimes we must accept
      Whatever has to be,
But God gave us tears
      For a reason don't you see.

Tears of joy or pain,
      For us He is always there,
'Cause in the midst of all storms,
      He really does care.

THE WARMTH OF HIS LOVE

Lord, wrap us in the warmth
     of your sweet love,
Give us peace and joy
     and strength from above.

Help us express that love to others
     as we go along,
As we feel your warmth,
     put within our hearts a lovely song!

HIS COVENANT, HIS VOW

I'm nestled safely underneath His wings,
I'm happy within for my heart sings,
I'm at peace because of His heavenly protection,
I'm saved as a result of His resurrection.

Yes! I'm saved, peaceful, happy, safe;
I am truly blessed,
And I have an invitation to a supper,
To me personally addressed.

So, I'll remain safely nestled
Underneath His wings for now,
'Cause, He's gonna rapture His own,
Yes! He'll keep His covenant, His vow!

OH!! THOSE DAYS GONE BY!!

Ever lived where the roof leaked
      when it would rain?
And all Mom's pots and pans
      played a wet tune in vain?

Ever lived where you could read
      the comics right off the wall?
Or shopped Sears & Roebuck
      in an outbuilding that was narrow and tall?

Ever knocked an apple out of a tree
      and enjoyed every single bite you ate?
Ever picked berries and forgot about the chiggers
      until it was too late?

Ever tried to 'help' Mom by trying
      to ring the chicken's neck?
And found you couldn't finish it
      And Mom gave you much more than a peck?

Ever stirred up a big batch of muddy,
      muddy mud pies?
And got it all over yourself,
      even in your eyes?

Ever made a playhouse using
  all of Mom's broken dishes?
Ever looked at the stars
  and made lots and lots of wishes?

Ever slept three in a bed
  and you got the middle?
Or slept at the foot of the bed
  just because you were little?

Ever ate beans and taters one day
  and taters and beans the next?
And then Sunday maybe you got a chicken leg
  or maybe just the neck?

Ever went down a path
  and got a bucket of water so fresh?
And along the way picked flowers
  just for Mom's dress?

All these things I've listed
  were in simpler times gone by!
But, people, we've come a long, long way
  —my, oh my, oh my!!

BUT, NOWADAYS, WE SIGH!!

Nowadays houses are so tight
        we can't hear what goes on outside?
And Mom's pots and pans go for days without a drop of water
        'til they're parched and dried!

Our comics are written daily
        while a real antic of life just grows and grows!
Our 'outbuilding' is now an 'in building'
        and Sears and Roebuck have turned up their nose!

As for apples, it's advised to eat one
        every day to be forever healthy!
So!! Apples off the tree and berries off the vine
        —we were plain ole wealthy!

As for that chicken neck stuff—
        I did that for real and really tried!
And felt sorry for that ole chicken;
        I ran away and cried!

In my childlike eyes, those mud pies
        in Mom's dish really looked delicious!
But, they just didn't have enough seasoning
        to make them nutritious!

As for those stars, I wished and wished
        and they shined and shined!
But, as a child's impatience took over,
        my heart just pined and pined!

As for sleeping in the middle and at the foot of the bed,
        I've done both you see!
Didn't really matter 'cause it was good
        to be just two friends and me!

Now, the taters and beans and the beans and taters
      still stand true today!
'Cause by throwing in some cornbread and onions,
      not much any better, I say!

The chicken leg and the neck seem
      to be things of the past for sure!
With so many fast food places,
      our kitchens think we've gone on tour!

Most of us don't even have a bucket,
      let alone a path leading to a spring!
When we need water, we just reach over
      and turn that turning thing!

We don't pick flowers for Mom anymore—
      she wouldn't know what to do!
We just call the flower shop and they fix and deliver
      and Mom still cries 'boo hoo'.

You'll notice, it took more words to write about today
      and our new time saving ways!
But to walk yesterday's path (just for a little while), we would
      have plenty of time for simple things of the 'good ole days'!

But!! Just think for a moment, these two different 'times'
      have one thing in common that we can see!
Our Lord and Saviour has always been there
      to supply each and every need for you and me!!

NOW, LOOKING TO THE FUTURE

Looking to the future, things like tight houses and pots and pans
     will expire—we may shed a tear,
And maybe comics, 'out' and 'in' buildings
     and even Sears and Roebuck will just simply disappear.

Perhaps we won't have apples or berries
     or even food to enjoy; we as this human race,
Food replaced by a pill? My! My!
     Sure hope I'm gone before that takes place!

We probably won't have chicken necks to ring
     or any clean mud for mud pies,
But, that won't be a problem, 'cause most children
     will have a computer glued to their eyes.

As for the stars, they'll still be in the sky
     if we can see through the smog,
We'll probably be 'beamed' from place to place
     —we won't even need to jog.

Now, taters and beans with cornbread and onions
     —a delicacy I don't want to give up,
And you know? We may not even have coffee
     to put in our coffee cup.

Our houses will be 'spaced out' like the 'Jetsons',
        full of buttons for us to push,
You know? Things like spring paths and buckets,
        flowers for Mom and trees—we won't even have a bush.

All these things come under a heading of progress
        and maybe that's true,
But, seems as progress has progressed,
        we have zero time—me and you.

Time to enjoy simple things like sitting in the shade,
        whittling or an afternoon nap,
Yes, things like watching a sunrise or sunset or
        holding a grandchild on our lap.

But!! Someday—all these things
        will be things of the past,
'Cause Jesus Christ our Saviour is coming back
        to claim His own at last.

Then we'll be rejoicing
        and we won't have anything to worry about,
Yes! Yes! He's coming in the clouds
        and we're leaving here with a shout!!

A FAITHFUL PRAYER

God, I know
    You are there;
Yes, you are there,
    And you care.

Sometimes, you seem
    To hide and wait,
Perhaps you wait for me
    To move with faith.

Like a child learns to walk,
    I must make a step,
To admit my need for You
    And Your help.

Sometimes, I have doubt
    But then I see the cross,
And know You're still in charge,
    And all is not lost.

GRACE TO FACE

He gives me grace to face
     what lies ahead of me,
Praise God for grace to face
     everything that has to be.

I don't know what I would do
     without my Lord and Saviour,
'Cause without grace to face
     I wouldn't be in His favor.

All my life He has supplied grace to face
     whatever came along,
I know His supply never runs out;
     it's abundance gives me a song!

WON'T YOU ACCEPT HIM?

Friend, God loves you
      no matter what you've done,
He can make your life complete
      if you come to Him through his Son.

You must ask forgiveness for your sins
      and have a humble heart,
Yes, just kneel at the foot of the Cross
      and He will do His part.

You'll never again be
      the same person that you are,
Yes, following Jesus Christ
      is the best way by far.

So, won't you accept Him
      as your Saviour this day?
Just as He leads others,
      He will lead you, come what may!

A PRAYER FOR EACH DAY

Lord, as the sun shines today,
    Shine thru me,
Help me to walk and talk
    In a way pleasing to Thee.

In those times of feeling low,
    Give me a peace within,
Make me aware of my weakness,
    Keep me from willful sin.

Help me stand face to face
    With that tricky old devil,
Give me a determination
    Not to stoop to his level.

Turn my thoughts to your ways,
    Give me humble boldness to stand,
And, Lord, no matter how low I feel,
    Help me hold on to your hand.

Take control of my tongue,
    Don't let me argue or myself defend,
Help me give You my problems
    And the victory I'm sure to win.